more praise for

LEADWOOD

I've had the pleasure of reading Dan's work for well over two decades and am in awe of his ability to effortlessly take the reader through a gamut of emotions and leave them pondering about how they ended up where they did. His candor coupled with his ability to address challenging subject matter reminds us how vital poetry is in this world.
—Rebecca Schumejda
author of Our One Way Street

These poems are wild, tender, sacred, profane, heartfelt, gorgeous, sorrowful, and powerful. I hope the fact that he keeps writing them saves Dan's life. God bless him. God help him make it through.
—Steve Henn
author of Indiana Noble Sad Man of the Year

When Dan Crocker walked the ghost-filled hallways of Leadwood High School, nobody would've ever thought that he would one day become the town's most famous man, well, they should've known. Someone once said that everyone who came out the 90s small press scene was a genius, if that's true Dan Crocker is our king, somewhere up in Heaven Ferlin Husky is singing soulful dusty ballads about him as we speak and that seems only right.
—John Dorsey
author of Dying like Dogs

'Nothing grows here,' the opening poems tells us, but the full collection says otherwise. Part elegy, part ode, part scathing critique, Leadwood is always surprising in its honesty and unflinching in its observations. Crocker reminds us that a poet's eye can find beauty (create beauty) even in a place covered in sewage.
- Jenny Yang Cropp
author of Not a Bird or a Flower

LEADWOOD:
new and selected poems
1998-2018

poems by
Daniel Crocker

Stubborn Mule Press
Devil's Elbow, MO
stubbornmulepress.com

Copyright (c) Daniel Crocker, 2018
First Edition 11 7 5 3 2 1
ISBN: 978-1-946642-71-4
LCCN: 2018957924

Design, edits and layout: Jason Ryberg, Jeanette Powers
stubbornmulepress@gmail.com
Cover Image: Jon Lee Grafton
Title Page Image: Jeanette Powers
Author photo: Margaret Bazzell-Crocker

All rights reserved. No part of this publication may be reproduced or transmitted in any form or by any means, electronic or mechanical, including photocopying, recording or by info retrieval system, w/out prior written permission from the author.

contact Daniel Crocker: buktrouble@gmail.com

For Margaret, always.

CONTENTS

Introduction by Nathan Graziano

Where We Come From	1
City of Bones	5
I Don't Write Political Poems	9
The Hulkster	12
People Everyday	15
Brutal	36
Spanking Diane Sawyer	40
My Old Landlord and Tim Allen End Up in a Sitcom Together	42
Growing Up	44
He-Man, You Smarmy Bastard	46
The Blonde	47
Dear Lion-O	49
Elton and George	51
Welcome to Fantasy Island	53
Elmo Goes Emo	55
My Mother Calls	56
A Dream of Siblings	58
The Devil	60
Sorry, Richie	62
The Incredible Hulk Goes Grocery Shopping After Taking a Handful of Klonopin	74
Hulk Meets Moloch	75
The Incredible Hulk Tries to Write a Poem	77
Bruce Banner Wakes Up Hungover	79
Bruce Banner's Intrusive Thoughts	80
Bruce, Betty and Hulk Figure It All Out	82
Dawn	83
Paper Anniversary	84
Sestina McRib	86
The Night I Met Larry Brown	88

How Me and Lord Byron Got our Grooves Back	91
Threw My I Ching	94
Stigmata	96
I Wish My Wife Liked Me Half as Much as She Likes *Fargo*	98
I Used to Be Someone's Favorite Eclipse	100
If I was Magic	102
I Married a Sling Blade	104
C is for Cookie	106
Ashley's Poem	108
The Unclean	111
Gemini	113
Abomination	115
Gemini	118
River	120
The City	122
Gemini	123
Missouri	124
Family	127
Halloween	129
Gemini	130
City	131
River	132
Father	133
Jeffry	134
The River	135
Halloween	136
How Many Miles Must I Run before I Beat Depression	138
South 55	140
Some Fava Beans	143
Eat	145
The Berryman Thud *(A Dramatic Monologue)*	147

They Haven't Called It a Complex in Forty Years	149
The Great British Baking Show	152
All Hail Walmart	154
Why We Kill Ourselves	155
What 'Possums Want You to Believe	156
What Spider-Man Dreams Of	157
Oscar the Grouch	159
Mania Makes Me a Better Poet	160
Jazz	162
Dinged	168
You Better Fucking Believe There's a Monster at the End of this Book	170
In Response to the Article "10 People to Rid Yourself of before the New Year"	172

Acknowledgments
Author Bio

Introduction to *Leadwood*

I was visiting the poet Lindsay Wilson in Bakersfield, California, the first time I came across Dan Crocker's work. It was 1999, and I was teaching in Las Vegas, a tenure that only lasted a year. That year, however, I had begun submitting and publishing my work in small press 'zines, which is how I met Lindsay, who was editing the print journal Unwound.

At Lindsay's house in Bakersfield, he had veritable truckload of rare small press journals and chapbooks. Among the chapbook pile, there was a slick-looking perfect-bound book of poems published by the oddly-named Green Bean Press. The book was titled *People Everyday and Other Poems*.

"Check this out," Lindsay said, handing me his copy. "Dan Crocker is amazing."

I looked at the cover and laughed, a laugh that contained some genuine amusement mixed with a pinch of jealousy. On the cover, a man with a goatee was wearing a hairnet, a bathrobe and a floral-printed nightgown. He was standing over a stove, cracking an egg into a frying pan. The kitchen was small, cloistered with a cartoon-ish cutting board leaning against the back of the stove. On the counter was a shot glass, and in the background, there was a bottle of something that looks like the whiskey.

The man on the cover—who I would later discern was the poet himself—had a cigarette dangling from his mouth, an abundance blush painted on his cheekbones and a wedding ring. "What the fuck is this?" I asked Lindsay, holding up the book.

"Read it," he said.

And I did. And by the time I finished the elegiac poem for his deceased brother "Sorry, Ritchie"—a poem I still contend is one of Dan's best—Crocker had a new fan.

Full disclosure: Dan and I are now best friends. So this is not going to be some aloof academic deconstruction or pretentious analysis of Dan's poetry. The short version of the long and discursive story of our friendship is that after reading People Everyday, I began corresponding with Dan. Later, Green Bean Press would publish my own books, and eventually, the publisher Ian Griffin and I would drive to Michigan to meet Dan and his family. Dan and I hit it off immediately, and the rest was proverbial history.

We've been best friends for well over a decade, and now here I am, on a sweltering summer night, nearly twenty years since Lindsay first handed me that book, writing the introduction to my best friend's collected poems. In retrospect, I'd argue that everything you're about to read in this robust and impressive collection can be gleaned from the cover of that first full-length book.

Let's begin with the fact that Dan is dressed in drag. One of the great strengths of Dan's poetry is his uncanny ability to self-deprecate and laugh at himself. His humor is dark and sardonic and bombproof, as you'll see in the persona poems where he writes from the points-of-view of The Cookie Monster, Elmo, Skeletor from He-Man, Hulk Hogan and The Incredible Hulk, among others. Yet Dan's never fishing for a cheap chuckle; there's always something looming behind the humor, something dark and ominous that forces us to see strains of ourselves and our world behind the voices of these characters.

And behind that floral nightgown, there is a man who has constantly and bravely confronted the complexities of human sexuality. One of the traits of a great poet is the ability to make their selves vulnerable on the page, something refreshing and utterly un-teachable. You see this in poems like "Sorry, Ritchie", "People Everyday" and "They Haven't Called It a Complex in Forty Years". Dan intuitively understands that sexuality and gender roles are far from cut-and-dry, and he has been exploring these themes long before the discussion made it into the mainstream.

There's also something about the kitchen on the cover of People Everyday, the fact that it is so small and cloistered seems to suggest something about the suffocation of growing up and living in the small and unconscionably neglected old Missouri lead-town that is this collection's namesake—this "City of Bones". I would never suggest that Dan is trying to become a mouthpiece for the wracked and forgotten denizens of Leadwood—poets don't typically make much of a collective dent in our culture. But Dan understands the struggles of poverty and alcoholism (there's that whiskey bottle and shot glass), the abuse and drug addiction that marries it in thousands of similar small towns throughout the United States. This is evidenced from the first poem "Where We Come From" and explored throughout his work. However, Dan is not eliciting the reader's sympathy, rather their concern while pointing out that the "population [of] 1,200" is much more than a census number. These are real people.

Finally, what might seem like minutia on the cover is far from it as you navigate this collection: Dan's wedding ring. Anyone who has ever been married understands the struggles and the joys of making a life and a family with someone else. In "Ashley's Poem", Dan writes adoringly and heartbreakingly of the day his daughter was born, and he offers similar tributes to his wife Margaret in pieces like "Paper Anniversary" and "If I Was Magic". But don't expect saccharine sentimentalism. Dan has been married long enough to know such sentiments are cheap and instead he confronts the confusion and the hard work it takes to keep love going, to keep each other close.

I could conclude—as Dan has asked me to do—with something that could be blurbed on the back cover of this book: "Dan Crocker is a brave and important poetic voice that the 21st Century desperately needs" or "Crocker's great strength lies in how bravely and unflinchingly he confronts a sad, crooked and beautiful world." Both are true. But I won't give him that satisfaction.

Instead, I'd like to go back to that afternoon in Bakersfield, California, when Lindsay Wilson handed me his book. In handing me Dan's poems, he unknowingly introduced me to my best friend. Selfishly, it was one of the greatest gifts I've ever received.

Now it's my turn to give this to you.

—Nathan Graziano

Where We Come From
(Leadwood, Missouri pop. 1,200)

Matt lit a joint here once
driving beneath the outstretched arms of dying trees

The moon shone through in jigsaw puzzles
that we could never quite figure how to put together

Gravel crackled like leaves in fire
underneath the weight of tires and restless boys

And we scattered beer cans
in no particular order
across the floorboard
left at the sides of dirt roads

Annette had just broken it off w/ him
and he beat drums out on the dash
a blue bandana stretched tight
across his forehead

And the September air held the smell of burning trash
in the tips of her fingers somewhere far away

We liked the looks of our faces basked blue in electric
light the call numbers of a station we had not tuned to

Eventually high we rode back into town
two cowboys and a whiskey bottle between us.

II.

Old timers sit staring from their porches

no job to wake up to they watch potholes for clarity
A future for the boys passes on the tailgate of a Ford
ripens like a soft apple and falls away

Graduation 1991
we ride past the foundation of the old movie house
burnt to the ground in '52
Glen once stood naked there on a dare

A fake gold cap is twisted from a bottle of cheap
champagne handed palm to palm w/ no comment

Mandy passed out hours ago
her jeans smooth against her thighs
bone white under the moon
we whooped it up like only good old boys can do.

III.

The hair on our hands spout into rusted wires
Matt's teeth gleam beneath a snarled lip

Voices of the wind
lost in the hunt
are never heard
from again.

IV.

The chat dump is waste spilled
from the great lead mines of the 20's

Our grandfathers worked there grew old and died
and left our grandmothers w/ nothing

The chat dump broods over this town like a tomb
(sand and lead dust pumped from the earth)

Its sprawl is endless
a hand clenched tight
it covers everything here
like a curse

It choked our fathers
it choked our grandfathers

Sometimes men in suits come from the city
and test our water

We know it's not safe
but what can you do?

My mother sat me down in it
when I was an infant

She cast her spells under the toenail moon
chanted words men were never meant to hear
and let me be
the curse of the wild falling somewhere between us

The chat dump is where fires burn until dawn
kegs empty quickly
and twenty-somethings w/ nothing else to do
ponder the possibility of iron and steel

The chat dump is a desert
in the heartland
Budweiser cans and cigarettes
stomped out in mid-smoke

Nothing grows here

The chat dump the half-shell of some cosmic turtle

Matt and I tried to climb it once
in his Daddy's Chevy
halfway up the tires stuck
then, backing down, we nearly rolled her to our deaths.

City of Bones
"the worst thing we've ever seen"
—Robert Bowcock, environmental investigator and colleague of Erin Brockovich (Speaking of Leadwood, Missouri)

I.

The bones broken
bleached cages
just down the street
the new weeds grow
a strange green

The solution to cover lead
w/ more lead from a town
not much better off than we are

When that didn't work they
sprayed it down w/ sewage

It's safe, they promised

And the bones grew to dandelions
and we were thankful
to find femurs, ribs bent
to smiles, bits of teeth
tumors spreading into
the marrow of our lives

The shit brought in from the Livestock
Sale Barn, the port-o-potty company
full of hypodermic needles biting

And then

Well, and then there was nothing
not even the sound of our cancers
only the weight of lead
in our blood and minds

This is what our fathers died for
we said.

II.

I said:

The Company left us
here where the chat dumps loom
like tombstones
left us like pigs w/out tits to suck

I said:

The Company decided
lead was no longer viable
and left us w/ it
an illness

I said:

An illness
we're all so very sick
it doesn't really matter anymore
what the men in suits from safer cities

say I said:

When they got around to it
they hauled in dirt w/ less lead

to cover what we already had and when that didn't work
they covered our town in literal shit

Months later we were still
picking out bones and teeth from the dirt

In some yards after the rain
had washed it away
we were left w/ piles of bones
cattle they said

It's safe and the needles
no one is ill, no one is sick

Our grandfathers won't speak of it
won't utter an ill word toward The Company
that fed them gave them something to do w/ their
backs and hands.

III.

What I really mean is this:
        the lead runs deep
        the dark waters
        the tumored fish
        the rough hands
        run deep
        Robbie killed himself
        Mike killed himself
        Buck killed himself
        on and on

It's so simple
our town is small
there's no money.

IV.

We live in shit
        we vote Republican
        we pound our Bibles
        eat at McDonald's
        drive big trucks
        we drink a lot
        we fight a lot
        we fuck a lot
        and pray a lot for salvation

The lady across the street
finally took down her *Jesus
is coming soon* sign
there's glory in the blood

We were all so busy
waiting on Armageddon
we never noticed
it was already here.

I Don't Write Political Poems
(written on the eve of a government shutdown)

We fed our kids
fish sticks
and we ate corn dogs
we knew it was poison

Sometimes we didn't eat
my mother fed me fat noodles
in watered-down tomato sauce
covered in spices from a plastic bottle

After three or four days
I imagined them worms writhing in blood

In sixth grade
I had a cough for six months
but my only doctor trip
was for scabies

They itched in hard
red welts, living there
they were contagious
a poor people problem

My grandmother
read us the Bible at night instead
instead of what
no one ever said

I don't write political poems because
I'm no expert
on the economy or budgets
or cost cutting measures

I am an expert
on being poor

Making a box of Kraft
Macaroni and Cheese stretch
like bloody fingers across a white
plate in a white apartment

There's some money now
and we give what we can
or so we say
but when I'm writing this

There's electricity T.V.
an open can of Diet Coke
half-empty and flat
that I'll throw away

How many people
could I feed on what I
spend on Diet Coke
a number

Still others wait
while I wonder what
could have been done
w/ all the money

Spent on beer
and whiskey
and cigarettes
all the cool poet tricks

Still others hoard cash
in the name of Jesus
but it's hard to eat a tank
and bullets don't make good doctors

Sometimes the noodles had hamburger
most of the time they didn't

Out of habit
my sister waited
to go to the doctor
and now it's too late

                Let's shut her down, boys!

    I see my mother standing
    in front of an open window

    It's summer
    she's wringing
    a dishtowel
    dry in her hands.

The Hulkster

Knees crumbled
like blue cheese and my back
always hurts. But when
my wife left and took all my money
what could I do?
I worked

I mean I wrestled
I'm not a rocket scientist
for Christ's sake
I'm Hulk fucking Hogan

She ended up dating
a guy who looks just like
I did the in '80s

He's 19. That's weird
right?

I've never wanted so badly
to be young again

The '80s were good
Ronald Reagan, White Snake, Molly Ringwald
the old red white and blue flying in every other yard
I
body slammed Andre
the Giant. I dropped my big leg
on The Iron Sheik. It was
a metaphor, brother

I was the Hulkster

Now I have nothing
a trunk full of bandanas
a daughter who looks just
like her mother. It's hard

Even I can't Hulk up out of everything

Me, the original real American
destitute, living in a one room apartment
w/ a television that only picks up CNN
I'm lying so still. Are all those
droned daughters my daughters, too?

The blood and bone of my daughters?
The missing limbs of my daughters?
The fathers who are gone forever
are they me?

I was made to hurt people

In the end, it didn't matter
who I worked for. They're all
the same suits, the same greased up
hair, the same fat white smiles

It has all run so very wild

Don't feel sorry for me
I got my cut
and at night I still say my prayers
and eat my vitamins
all of these beautiful
pills for pain.

Government Cheese

I, too, was poor
and ate government cheese
and squirrel
and other things

People forget
what a trailer park really is
a ghetto
bathtub meth
your cousin
coming down w/ it
the hook

The kind of place
it's hard to write
yourself out of

The taste
of government cheese

Government cheese
broken down Buicks
the place the wind can pick up
on a whim
and wipe clean
and ain't nobody
gives a goddamn.

People Everyday

I.

People everyday
    turn into what
        they were not meant to be
            made into but
            were forced
to be made into what they
were meant to be

What other people want them to be
    to zombies
        to machines
        to madmen
            foaming Lucifers

People everyday
    troubled
        become addicted
            clasp
rage tightly between walled teeth
knocking over friends
    planting
        dying
            vacant

People everyday are connected
    by eyes to screens
by fingers melted to letters
    are by knobs, by switches
bound by silicone contracts

Eaten

        cancer
            away
have ecstasy orgies
    on leave from the military
        lie in bed w/ cheeks spread
scream
    fuck me fuck me

People everyday
    are lonely
are afraid
   losing children/childhood
taking last breaths
are driving 14 hours
    to Missouri
        from Florida
getting shot at
    only to find no lover
        and return to Florida
two days later
w/ parents crying and wondering
what went wrong?

People everyday
    masturbate in parking lots
are
    dancing
like a string on a fan
    alone

People everyday
    have seen better times
are
    struggling through wrinkles
someone pulled their drawstring
    while wondering

if they are attractive
        and who their lover has fucked tonight

People everyday
        are losing their hair
                clinging like tile to life;
not their own
                no longer loved
lift the bottom of the bottle
        to Jesus

People everyday
        are giving dick sucks
behind decayed buildings
        right in your home town
               are
sharpening drill bits
while
        hot grease splatters
blisters over hands and face
                are
blowing themselves up
                trying
to smoke pot
        in a freezer full of gasoline

People everyday
        are
                living in cars
gaining weight
                attracting disease
putting thin steel into their dark veins
soaking from 3 straight days of speed
        reading books by
Kant Sartre Hume and God
                losing faith

sitting behind the Baptist church
God structure w/ hooded woods
and imaginary eyes closing
    open-handed
        in on him
hanging
    up signs proclaiming *Jesus is coming soon*
to die
    7 years later
never to see the prophecy fulfilled

People everyday
    dye their hair because
        they know how physically
            repulsive they must be
shave eyebrows
    and wonder
        what to do
            w/ the rest of their lives
take to tie-dyed boxes
    because they
can no longer afford school
    and can no longer afford to be cattle

Drink Everclear straight
    while huffing gas ghost
    convulsing
on the floor
    razor blades
        training
through their blood stream
veins
clanking to painful halts
at every joint
let themselves
    be locked in a cage

by shiny boys beautiful
    be fucked in the ass
in front of a crowd in New Orleans
    while getting nipples pierced
at a late-night party
    and claim they have nothing left to live for
fantasies fulfilled
lie
    dusty
        in basements
shaking w/ the fear
the locust are coming back

We are
    people everyday.

II.

People everyday
    alive for nothing
wander aimlessly   in and
  out
of jobs   seeking nothing   for
    they have no eyes
die   via
        Ebenezer Scrooge
  alone and afraid like babes
w/out   even
a   Christmas   past
to hold onto
    or the memory
of ever having spare dollars

Party w/ death solutions
   when   taking

it anymore
is not
    an   option
and only
show for it
    spit
down a hairless chin
    and a bloody nose
swallow muscle relaxers
    give head
to   puss-faced
queer boys   and let
their
fiancé   sleep   alone
  on the broken glass of
their picture   frame
deciding if this
    fun
is taking   too long.

Love vodka
    when
meth   is short
    in   Missouri
and   New Orleans
is too
far
  away
in some
    absent-minded withdrawal
throw junk ceramics
    at
the door of a 3
year old girl   only to be
    punched   out by
a man

w/ a wife   who kisses
too much
'cause   after all
    that's
what friends   are
for

Grow short
    and old
at 50   and slowly
squander   a life's
savings   when
    gambling's excitements
can only defeat
    the boredom of gray hair
  nowhere to turn
    when the sheriff knocks
on the door
    old woman off to prison
found the found out poet mother

Find
    lumps in their stomachs
when they can't eat
    still refuse
to
 let
    doctors
shove clear plastic black fluid
tubes up their   asses
to test
  only to test

Thank you, Missouri

Contemplate

    early   retirement
from   all of this
   but the health insurance
comes in handy

Drive drunk   and fast
away from
    their nuclear families
wishing
   a brush
w/   the pretty pale girl
in   the   back seat

Fuck   whoever come who may
   after   years   of
love
and abuse   and   the
record for   most dysfunctional   relationship
   then
  writing letters
afraid   and
wishing for it all
back

Decide   to   be married
   in the middle
of   a one night stand
     two   lonely   bodies
one
yes
to   more than
   are you coming?

Take their   dicks
   into   armed   forces
watch

```
        drill     sergeants
eat      puke
cry     for help
        when      they
can't    be     allowed
          to   paint pretty pictures
   of make-believe women
anymore

Publish         poetry
      no      one will ever read
    suckers
from the     first spiritual  moment
of conception

Watch    the     birth
of their first        born
       w/ wonders
of
   will it look like me
what sperm created this
and    oh won't    pharaoh
kill
          them all
get    their-tubes-tied
       w/ no reluctance
and      smile    like     a fish
      w/     the     realization
that
they     may      now
                   freely   fuck
   their    husband's       friends
        while
planning
        a
way
```

    out

Let   sleep   come
    dreaming   of
gnawing   insects   at   hearts
minds
    souls
sweat   toss
14   hours   in
   bed
3   hours   of
   sleep
pills   please
don't let them wake up
       tomorrow's another day.

III.

And America's streets are full of its bards
homeless   hungry
and willing to write for food
and people everyday like it that way

And we are going to work in shoe factories
bicycle factories
and factories for toy cars
and people everyday are glad to eat another week

And we run our hands through walls the cows aren't
coming home
and between China and Russia and everything else
people everyday have nothing left to fight about anymore

And people everyday are more than happy
we get drunk toast our heads under

hot faucets shake under shadow of dawn and people
everyday are wishing the divorce would go through

And we run from job to job work 2-10 at one
rush a burger and work 11-6 at the other
and people everyday make payments on new cars
America is joining channel 7 w/ a donut and speed

And
meth meth meth meth meth meth meth meth meth meth
and people everyday hope the new talk show host has
their   answers   this   time

And good friends are kicking the junk dying of AIDS
and putting bullets through their heads
and people everyday are letting this happen
and we make minimum wage spend it on beer and food

Hope the baby makes it through the winter hope for HUD
and kill cockroaches
and people everyday say
it just doesn't get any better than this

And the children all over the world are thin bones in plastic
and the children in Leadwood cry in the night
but no one hears their calls through the echo of fallout bombs
or sees them through the blood pouring from their own heads

And the T.V. offers 1-800-HOPE
meanwhile America's children play cowboy unload their guns
and fight their own wars
and people everyday try hard to ignore

People everyday have passed out at the bar w/ its bills unpaid
and we've psycho-babbled ourselves into a disease
analyzed our last strands of hope to early death
and the rivers flow w/ beer cans and the mountains w/ needles

And people everyday
wonder
are you dysfunctional
or am I dysfunctional?

IV.

And sometimes I'm in love w/ Missouri
where the rivers are flowing glass
and the sky lies naked and spread eagle
and friends dance in and out
like dreams drunk on wine
and we call each other by our real names
our forbidden god names
our parents never dared speak
and we touch our bodies together
and breathe in the breath of each other
and our skin is our skin
and our sweat is our sweat
and the Mississippi echoes
and the blue jazz of timeless thought
and old men sit on paint peeled porches
and drink a beer
and it is still safe for children to play in the street
and our blood is our blood
and our pain is our pain
and our love is our love.

V.

People Everyday suicidal!
People Everyday psychopathic!
People Everyday lonely!
People Everyday in my ass!

People Everyday lips on dick!
People Everyday shooting head!
People Everyday tragic angels!
People Everyday gah gah gah!
People Everyday 'fraid of queerboys!
People Everyday rot in ground!
People Everyday don't know nobody!
People Everyday is!
People Everyday hah hah hah!
People Everyday gonna kill somebody!
People Everyday manic depressive!
People Everyday politically correct!
People Everyday Lordy Jesus!
People Everyday me me me!
People Everyday barefoot in winter!
People Everyday sleep in piss and glass!
People Everyday fuckin' somebody!
People Everyday worthless!
People Everyday don't know no better!
People Everyday frustration!
People Everyday itsy bitsy!
People Everyday just watchin' T.V.!
   Goddamn you people everyday!
People Everyday Gods!
People Everyday crying saints!
People Everyday beautiful addicts!
People Everyday mine!
People Everyday nothing!
People Everyday everything!
People Everyday big universe!
People Everyday make me hard!
People Everyday bang bang bang!
People Everyday bang bang bang!
People Everyday!
   Bang! Bang! Bang!

VI.

Beautiful are people everyday
        old men and women stroll hand
in hand
c'mon, you've seen it

Homeless
        sleep well
and wash the windshields of Porsches
and Mercedes
   thank Jesus for that dollar, brother

Aging poets
        move from New York
breathe crystal air
where the beer tastes good

Mothers-to-be
        light up
find god   and hate
the baby

Children
        pick their flowers
watch them rot
but know the spirits
        grow and grow again
no matter how many lawn mowers
   roar that way
   get old and forget

Hard bodied young men and women
        everyday fall in love
if only for minutes at a time

Millions watch the comets come
        the stars fall
the sky burn   the land soak
and their stomachs feel
their place in this cycle
        flicker out
like one hit wonders

Ah,
does this poem go on and on
        let it march for eternity
  wearing different bodies
  singing different stanzas.

VII.

You can never really know
the gaudiness of suicide
until you've been right there
w/ it
the Las Vegas
splotches of red and brain
glittering off white walls
or the utterly pathetic
melodrama
in finding a body
surrounded by candles
hanged in a tuxedo
but mostly it is the after-effect
        the ripples of excitement
        the behind back whispers in town
        the knowing winks
        the macabre speculation
        the game of dress up
        the church basement dinner parties

          the way they strut
          the funeral parade
          the heaven/hell debate
          the look on people's faces
one of such importance
and the better you knew the victim
the more important you are
more importantly it brings
meaning to the community
as a whole
remember, it was even
in the newspapers

All the small towns
need big signs:

SUICIDE HERE: ONE WEEK ONLY

VIII.

(blank)   Look for a gun on sober nights
       wish my friends were here   wish I didn't
           suck the last of their memories and souls
               pick at their brains
put them on paper as organized ink stains
and I write about   loving them and I
write about hating them
           and I write about kissing them and I
write about hitting.

IX.

They caught your body
    (like a butterfly)

in a smooth plastic box

I couldn't believe it
   your beautiful body
smothered in roses
   so empty
in red silk
   nothing behind those (once)
mischievous eyes

Your (once) thin feminine hands
   clutching a small black bible
now swollen fat
   knuckles like an old man

I watched your little brother
   (only 13, the age I was
when my brother died)
   try to fix your hair
so that your bald spot
   didn't show
how cold could it have felt
   to his fingers?

I cried a little
   and only a little
   you were free
at least of heroin
   and the older men who
used your body
   for its childish looks
all our old friends were there
   dropping you kisses
and personal objects
   like valentines
so many red faces

Your dad (finally there)
   talked in a loud
drunk's voice to his buddies
   in the front row
about fishing
   and hunting deer
(was that in his voice when
   he fucked you?)

No one could save you

The preacher was a woman
   and I'm sure you liked that
your faith never wavered
   just your appreciation
of it

She talked of hope
   and the sense of peace
that she felt
   though she'd never met you

She stared at your mother
   and it made me wonder
what everyone could have been
   thinking

I missed the rough stubble of your
cheek when we kissed
your hard cock pressing against me
so
I left god out of it
despite what hypocrites say
   to believe in god
is to believe
   that you are burning in hell

(and after the hell you had here)

I can't.

X.

And people everyday shit fire shakin' their asses
    the gothic ritual to bring back the dead
and people everyday are growing roots deep into the earth
    promising themselves *tomorrow is another day*
and people everyday are in search of something spiritual
    in a world that has seen its gods forgotten
and people everyday are surfin' the internet tryin' to meet
    friends because real flesh and blood's grown cold
and people everyday sing the star spangled banner finally
    hoping to get it right this time

And people everyday are turning off the television
    turning off the television that gawd hath given
    looking at the world around them through windows
and they're tired of what they see
and people everyday have stopped going to church
    and started worshiping gods
and they feel the universe like a blanket around them
and people everyday have stopped blaming others
    and have taken the cross themselves

And the lawyers are out of jobs
and people everyday have closed down the grocery store
    started growing their own food
and we'll never go hungry again
and people everyday can feel me right now
    and they're singing along
and smiling at what we've done

And people everyday have shunned remote controls
        picked up books of poetry
and set the streets on fire
and people everyday put down those books and run naked
        through the woods and the thorns don't cut
        them anymore and they are thanking the caterpillar
and they are (   )
and people everyday cultivate their gardens
        and they finally know why

And someone said *hello* to their neighbor today
and people everyday have started walking to work
and the sky has uncovered itself and given its blessing
and now we all know what the stars are made of
and people everyday have said *enough is enough*

        And started playing the old games
and people everyday give up on technology
        and break the mass silence
and it is possible to talk again
and people everyday have un-invented nuclear power
        and keg gun powder
and the generations have all known peace

And people everyday join in late night communion
        w/ the elders of their suburban tribe
and leave knowing the grass will speak if they listen
and people everyday are crowded around fires
        just to keep dry to join souls not for vacation
and people everyday have come to one understanding
and they visit river banks w/ their sons

And daughters
and when they touch that cool water they know
        they're touching the hands and mouths of the world
and people everyday have seen the light

       come to understanding and quit the meager jobs
and so that is what the family looks like
and people everyday have thrown away blue and white pills

And have finally fucked the police
and people everyday rub their hands w/ the mantis
       make their music w/ the cricket and bull frog
and the tones of a thousand evolutions echo in our ears
and people everyday are turning off their lights
       touching their lovers and blazing their candles
and everyone is going to get a good night's sleep.

Brutal

"Let's have a gay night," he said.

"A gay night?"

Of course, we didn't know what he meant. I was eight and my cousin, Terry was nine. We were staying the night w/ our great-aunt and our 19-year-old cousin, Larry, who lived w/ her. Larry was very handsome, and he could almost dunk a basketball, which went a long way w/ us. He also seemed to like hanging out w/ us. Earlier, Terry and I (who grew up in the same house) had been playing army w/ him in our back yard. Larry was tall, lean, and dark-skinned.

Looking back on it thirty years later, I'm surprised, and a bit upset that I remember him as being so attractive.

"A gay night," he said. "We all do it. It makes us men. First, let's show our dicks to each other."

This is where coherency ends.

What I remember are flashes ... bits and pieces. Some of it, I didn't remember until a few years ago when Terry and I talked about it for the first time.

Terry and I were nervous. We laughed a lot. We finally pulled our dicks out. Larry's was hard as a rock, huge it seemed to me, surrounded by pubic hair. Terry's was just naturally big. Mine wasn't. So it, of course, became the butt of jokes for the night. It didn't help that I was fat. A little plump pig, which Larry seemed to actually like. After we'd pulled our cocks out and talked about them for a bit, Larry invited us downstairs.

Our great-aunt had one of those old-fashioned exercise machines down there. One w/ a limp, stained belt.

"Let's take turns putting our dicks on it and turning it on," Larry said. So we did. Somehow, this is the worst part of it. Has always been the worst part of it. Thinking back, which I try not to do, it's the monster in the basement. Dirty and stained. I knew even then that this was the turning point. There would be no going back after the monster. I even thought about stopping it then.

Other than this, we mostly just went to church together. Larry would sit beside us, smacking green apple gum, and asking as quietly if he could which girls in church we might fuck, if we had the chance. We thought that was really cool. He'd even ask us about his sister, who I had some sort of weird, 8-year-old crush on.

It got worse, of course. It was all about what we would do to him. Would we touch his balls? Would we take his dick in our mouth? I did. Hating it and liking it at the same time. I honestly can't remember what Terry did. I'm sure it was much the same.

When I titled this "Brutal," I expected it to be brutal. Other than a surreal poem I wrote and published in the late 90s, this is the only thing I've ever written about that experience. The poem dealt in symbolism. I told myself, *if I ever have the guts to write about it, it's going to be brutal.* It's going to be honest and detailed. The details, however, are like an impressionist painting. Parts of it, like the monster, are painfully vivid. Larry's white, white teeth. His beautiful body. The rest is images, textures, feelings. Feelings of guilt and desire all mixed up in one. The taste of his cock and how I remember it being both hard and somehow soft at the same time ... the way the skin of it followed my movements.

Whenever I would think about writing this, I'd think, *there's a book in it.* There's not. There are just these images. Whatever else there might have been, would be about the aftermath, and I've written about that over and over again.

The next morning, I woke up naked on the living room floor. Larry had uncovered me to show his sister. She was laughing at how fat I was. Terry was already ready for church. We didn't see Larry much after that. He decided we weren't really that cool to hang out w/ anymore. I guess we felt the same. The next time I remember seeing him was at my brother's funeral. He was still handsome. He had rented me a movie, Better Off Dead.

There's a lot to say about my brother and how, even though he knew nothing about this, he should have done something about it, but not here. The next time I heard about Larry, he had died in motorcycle accident. My hometown, Leadwood, kills a lot of people. I was happy he was dead. I'm not sure I am anymore.

For all of his talk about a gay night, Larry wasn't gay. Sometimes I am. And though I consider myself to have the most bleeding heart I've ever known, child molesters still make me scream out for the death penalty. That, however, is neither here nor there. That's just me still trying to defend myself for not stopping this. For not saying no to the monster.

When I was young, and I would feel like, or people would think, I was a really fucked up person, they would think maybe it was because my brother had died when I was thirteen. I'd let them. But it wasn't. It was this. This.

Terry and I were very, very drunk and in our 30s, at a bar, when I finally said something about it.

"You know why were so fucked up?" I asked.

"Larry," he said.

I nodded.

"The thing I most remembered," he said, "was Larry fucking you in the ass."

I hadn't remembered.

"You screamed like a pig," Terry said.

I remembered then. I remembered everything.

Hands and knees and pain.

Spanking Diane Sawyer

I want to spank Diane Sawyer
In fact, I'd pay upwards of
fifty dollars for it, at least
if she was wearing white cotton
panties

In my fantasy
I wonder
I stop and ask,
Is everything okay, Diane?

Yes, she says, *yes
just keep spanking*

*Do you remember
the safe word?*

She rolls her eyes
and wiggles her ass
annoyed w/ me

Look, I try my best
I really want to spank
Diane Sawyer

If I could just cut loose
for once

Instead, even here
in my fantasies
I stop

Those love taps just ain't

doing it for me, Diane says

I try to say something about my
mother
and a belt
and raw fat legs

Before I can though,
Matt Lauer is at the door
bald and bold and riding a Hog

They drive off together
somewhere, where I don't
know, but it's a rough, wild country.

My Old Landlord and Tim Allen End Up in a Sitcom Together

By accident
someone from Hollywood called
my old landlord for a reference

They knew from his voice
that he's real America
a regular Missouri guy
the kind folks can connect w/
so they coupled
him w/ Tim Allen

One will be the landlord
one the repairman

They'll put the show on
right after The Big Bang Theory

It will be a hit
manly men will do what manly men do
like fixing your sink two months
after you ask them to
or hiking the rent

People will start to wonder
what they ever saw in those
nerds from BBT to begin w/

All those Star Trek references
all those toys
Raj will anger them in ways
they can't or won't explain

They will begin to question everything:
        The Wonder Years
        Sanford and Son
        Will and Grace
        PBS

The foundation of their beliefs
will quake

They'll watch because
someone rich told them to

They'll watch until they
question their Gods.

Growing Up

I.

I saw the Cold War
hell, it was no Vietnam
but it was something

I saw Silence
equal Death
and stayed silent anyway

We watched "The Day After"
we watched "Roots"
every special news break
      we lost our faces
      shuddered
      sure of annihilation

They wanted to put Reagan's goddamned
face on a mountain and I
missed Haley's Comet for this.

II.

I was neurotic
in heat w/ religion
dry humping the word

When I sinned I prayed
Dear God, please forgive me
for all of my sins

When others sinned I prayed

Dear God, please forgive me
for all of my sins

If I thought of sin I prayed
Dear God, please forgive me
for all my sins

Sesame Street Ronald Reagan MTV
Sesame Street Ronald Reagan
and MTV
        what have you done
        to your weary
        ragged, holy boys?

He-Man, You Smarmy Bastard

You're not fooling anyone. You drug
half of us out kicking and screaming
Ram-Man, Extendar, Fisto,
you have to be kidding me

I see the way you and Beast Man
look at each other, the glances that pass in battle

Don't you have enough going on?
What w/ ruling Eternia
and the way Man-At-Arm's
mustache feels fatherly against your cheek

Who wouldn't want to see you
soaked in rain water?

Me. I have a fucking skull for a head
no one wants to hang out w/ the kid
who has a skull for a head. Let's put it this way
I didn't get invited to many parties

What choice did I have then but to be evil?
The Gods decided on a whim I would be your
eternal foe? Losing, always losing.
Could it be that simple?

Fuck you and that stupid cat you rode in on
let me into Grayskull you sleek, shirtless barbarian

You beautiful bourgeois man. Let me into
mother fucking Grayskull, you lovely bastard.

The Blonde
Winner of the first Gerald Locklin Award in Poetry

loves poetry
She watches me read
soaks in every word
She finds reasons to visit my office
to lean over
to say, *Dr. Crocker*

She's fit
I imagine her jogging
in spandex
There is no irony to it

This could be trouble, I think
but who am I fooling?

I'm an old poet well
past my prime in every way
I'm tired
I have drank too much
   smoked too many cigarettes
   blood pressure up, cholesterol bad
There is no way, in any way
I could satisfy this woman
or probably any woman

She would want to do things, I imagine
go places
live

I'm tired, I'd say
when we fucked she'd
have to be on top

and still, me red and out of breath
only half hard

I wanted a poet, she'd say
  and me trying to clean up my act
  no longer drinking beer or smoking cigarettes
  not even in secret
  reading, walking on a treadmill

And, of course, I have a wife
She's tired, too
having been married to a poet
all of these years

And when she's left unsatisfied
it hangs there heavy like a vow.

Dear Lion-O

So they went and un-gayed you in
their "re-imagining"
I'm sorry. It must be tough
Your abs really popped in that purple leotard

Of course, you cats had problems, too
You destroyed Thundera
crash landed on Third Earth
and immediately started taking over

What did that mutant ever do to you anyway?
History is written by the winners
I understand why you
sweep the colonialism under the rug

It's okay. We've all fucked up. But did they
have to make you younger, happier
give Cheetara bigger boobs
and make her a love interest?

A love interest for God's sake
We both know you're not interested
I know a little bit about rewriting my own history
Who hasn't given it a shot?

And God knows they've tried
to un-gay me as well
and believe it or not, a few folks
have even tried to un-straight me

You just keep going
holding onto the
Sword of Omens

like the phallic symbol it is

You'll always be the reason I love redheads
and try as they might
that's one thing
they can't take that from us.

Elton and George

The first time I kissed a man
we were at a straight party
alone in the kitchen
grabbing beers

The Elton John and George Michael
version of "Don't Let the Sun Go
Down on Me" came on the radio

We started to sing along
moving closer
to each other
hands clenched close
to our mouths
holding invisible
microphones

Something older than
Kentucky rain fell
between us

Then we kissed
full-tongued

We had to be careful
getting caught risked a beating.
It was like something
out of a goddamned movie

It was then I knew gay men
are better in both style and substance
at almost everything

The rest of the story
isn't so cute

It was 1991.
We were falling
in love in a small
town in Missouri

And two years later
he'd be dead
found hanged in his room
because, after all,
this was a small town
in Missouri in 1991.

Welcome to Fantasy Island

You are either God or a god
in your angel suit
I saw you make life from nothing

You even fought the Devil once
who, as I always suspected,
looked just like Roddy McDowall

Offer us love
offer us redemption
I dare you

No one's fantasy is ever:
> *I ran out of weed.*
> *I'm too fat.*
> *I have cancer.*
> *My husband is a real asshole.*

A quick perusal of Craigslist
shows that most fantasies have
nothing to do w/ dancing
w/ the late great Sammy Davis Jr.
> finding love or
> a child

but mostly have to do w/ nipple clamps
and bodily fluids

And you can't just *give* anyone their fantasy

Instead, it's a week of devastating
psychological torture
only to find that
our fantasies were w/in us

all along if we'd just
been able to see them

I briefly entertained the idea
that your island was sponsored by
the Koch brothers as a way
to convince poor people
they never really had it as bad
off as they thought

But, I've never seen any poor
people on Fantasy Island

I only see rich people
mostly white
I assume they
are Republicans

Then again, if you are God
why haven't any of them
freaked out about your Latin heritage?

Why hasn't Fox News declared Fantasy Island
a war on blue-eyed Jesus?
What the hell is Tattoo?
I need to know

By the time it's over
by the time you're done
toying w/ us
everyone wants off
this island

Even me. And I believe in
you, Mr. Rourke. I do.

Elmo Goes Emo

Elmo's soul is black as obsidian
Elmo's pain is only dampened
by the jagged cuts upon
Elmo's arms

Elmo made them w/ a beer bottle cap
Elmo wonders who can remember the sun
Elmo's heart torn like crepe paper

The stain on Elmo
cannot be washed away
not even by Tide
and Tide knows fabric best

Wind. Frigid. Cold. Winter.

Snuffleupagus has a trunk like a baseball bat
Elmo shouldn't have said that
Elmo's going to be gutted like a rat

Tickle Elmo?
Please
tickle Elmo
until Elmo can't breathe.

My Mother Calls

and says I need
to visit my sister
soon
My first thoughts
are selfish ones:
    No one tells me
    anything
    because I took my brother's
    death so badly as a boy

But I'm a grown man now
in middle-age
only a few years
younger than
the sister who used
to spank me w/
a giant metal spoon
Or better yet
pretend to so that
I didn't get a real
beating

Mom says:
    She's on so much pain
    medication now
    she doesn't always
    know where she's at

I feel the ground
under my feet
soaked w/ lead
I feel the last
        aging child

heavy on the heart
of my mother.
I make plans
w/ my wife
and daughters
to visit

    and all
    the
    anger
    in
    Leadwood, Missouri
    wells up
    right
    here
    in the
    final
    line
    of
    this
    goddamned
    poem

The true story
of Leadwood, Missouri is this:

    the ground that waits
    the blood heavy w/ lead
    the cigarettes we smoked
    and beers we drank
    the bullets we shot
    the bibles we kept
    the big company bucks
        someone
        somewhere
        makes.

A Dream of Siblings

I dreamed first of my sister

She couldn't speak
she was smiling

Young and beautiful
w/ long, straight red hair

She bopped me on the head
w/ a pen like little bunny foo foo

Then I was in a hearse
w/ my brother's old girlfriend
we were driving
through a gray, failing city

She was young. She tried crawling into the back seat
and I caught a glimpse of her striped panties

Shit, I thought, *this is it*
another sex dream about Vicki

But it wasn't

Your brother is still alive, she said
Your parents didn't tell you

I ask her to take me to him

He's on the top floor of an impossibly
tall apartment building

He's lying on a couch

he's covered in burn scars
his jaw is webbed skin, and I
can see his teeth and bloated tongue

He can't speak

It's been thirty years
It's me, I say. *It's Dan*
He weeps. He moans. He
tries to move, but can't
pain and silent pleading

When I wake I can't help but wonder
if this was a message from the afterlife

My sister, so devout
happy, impish and the pen?

I don't know

My brother who
carried a gun under the front
seat of his truck who died
driving drunk

in some kind of hell

Even though I gave up believing
in this shit years ago, I still wonder

Maybe I never gave up believing

Maybe, once having faith
no one ever gives up believing

Even if the things we believe in are horrifying.

The Devil

When I was young
I believed in the Devil
deeply

We believed in demon's
possession, that any stranger
could be an angel

We believed oil anointed
on the forehead just right
could crush cancer cells like June Bugs

Those that died either
lacked faith or couldn't
fight God's will

We stayed still in our beds
at night as spider stalk legs
crept down the hall

As shadows crept down the hall
we still believed in a divide between
the light and the darkness always at odds

We thought Jesus was coming soon

The Devil spoke to us through rock
and roll music if you knew how
to run your turntable backwards just right

When I was a boy
I prayed every waking
moment.

I prayed every waking moment

When I was a boy
I prayed every waking
moment I was so afraid of sin

I contemplate all this
over yet another mood
stabilizer

W/ pills like these
what choice do I have but to accept
the light and darkness as one

As if there is no difference
between what we do and say
or who we are and who we are.

Sorry, Richie

I.

I was eight years old
sitting at a beat up
typewriter—missing letters
once belonging to
our psycho-aunt
for a business class
never finished
that mom borrowed
because I told her
I wanted to write
a book about
my life

I wrote nine pages
hid them away like
the secrets of adults
but found you later
reading them, carefully

I was nervous
I may have cried
my soul may have
for a moment
wailed
before you said
I liked it

You lifted me
into the ceiling fan
heaven and told
me I had to responsibility

to keep going to always
keep going

All I could say
again and again
was that I was sorry.

II.

Eleven years old
I woke w/ the sun
to go to the station
w/ you
I wanted to drink soda
talk w/ the old man
who had bumps on his face
like a cucumber

For a few hours
there was no old man
gossip or repairs
so we talked
and
you talked to me
like I wasn't
just a dumb, fat kid

Remember how I used
to absorb the Bible
and beg you to read it
as well?

You said I did enough
reading for the both of us

You were probably right

I remember the rides
you took me on
in your old truck

You'd pick up Sprite
mix it w/ vodka
and sometimes I
would get a sip

Even then it tasted good

You'd have too much
play "Time in a Bottle"

Once, buzzed, I told
you Prince was a fag
you said you didn't care
if he sucked dick every night

I don't laugh like that anymore

There was the night
you came home drunk
crawled under the covers
w/ me
and told me about the girl who
had played the "Slobber
me Blues" on your meat horn.

I didn't know then
that a few years later
I would ask Glen—at
church camp—if
my brother had gone to heaven

or hell
and swearing you weren't drunk
even though we all knew you
probably were

How was I to know then
that I would end up w/ so many
cocks in my mouth
or that Glen was gay
or that I would come to love
Prince or that you kept a .357
under the seat of your truck

How?

Sometimes my friend Tom Moon
who we called "Tattoo"
for his fat head and because, Jesus
let's face it
he looked like Tattoo
would come to that station
w/ us knowing he was to die

We would drink sodas
make fun of Tom
and when we went in debt
and the station closed
Tom asked if it was
because of all those free
sodas we drank

Sometimes he would offer
money to make up for it
and I would take it
so I could eat lunch

And the next year
in an attempt to cheer me up
showed me a picture of a monkey
and said, "That's your brother"
before catching himself and chanting
Sister Sister Sister

I'm not going to hit you, Tom

Much later
Tom was put away
for trying to kill the mother
he thought had turned to
an insect

Now I think maybe Tom
was onto something
and if so
I'm sorry

III.

I remember the night
I was thirteen
you dressed in tattered jeans
and a sleeveless black Harley shirt

You kept telling me you
had three days "boof"
three days boof
from your late night
minimum wage security work

It seemed to us those three
days would last forever

didn't it

Am I reading too much into this

That same day
I told you a grease head
who once claimed he had bitten
a woman's nipple off and chewed
for hours like gum
offered me joints for a buck each

You told me to never do
the things you had done
it was like a country song

We had bologna sandwiches
canned vegetable soup
BBQ chips
and a contest to see
who could eat the fastest

I'll admit it now
you won

Though didn't I ask you
to take me for one more ride
just one more
before you left
to get a soda
to turn in small circles
like we once did
laughing at it all

And how was I to know
w/ how you used to scare me
driving madly or tapping on my

window at night
after you and Vicki had an argument

Or even w/ the dream the night
before where I was w/ you
not in your truck (which they
never let me see) but
your old Dodge

Should it have been enough
w/ you getting married the next month

How could I know
Mom would wake me up
the next day
my aunt would be screaming
at least he didn't suffer
it was all over quick
and he didn't suffer

Dad knelt beside me
I had never seen him cry before
he asked me what we were
going to do *for Christ's sake*

Had I known you weren't coming back
I would have fallen behind the tires
of your truck

I dream of that still
I would have shown you
everything I have written

I promise.

IV.

I sat at home (and
it's about time you knew this)
afraid to be alone
scared to be alone at night
eating something out of a box
Mom and Dad at work
the sun gone
and more scared to have them home
Mom's insane face
rain
staring up from dirt
rain
piss yellow eyes
rain
holes in earth
rain
you three days fresh
Missouri rain
and rising
Leadwood, Missouri rain
casket corner edged against the sun
rain
and rising
the second coming
of the first born

I never went back w/ her

The spot I had picked
was in back w/ stones
dates in the 1800s
Mom and Dad wanted
something up front
under a tree

They said it was just
a feeling

I dreamt of Mom coming
home flaking fingernails melting
scraping no-teeth and no-hands
ready to make me realize
the true confession
of your face
to make me know death
what it was like
in that split second when you know
that you are going to die
and there's nothing you can do about it
and there's nothing anyone can do about it

Was it scary

Scary as Dad's later warnings
that I would end up six foot
under the hill or
the later silence
or the nightmares for years
or the dreams you were alive
and we'd wrestle like we used to
and there would be no reason
for the kids at school
to feel sorry for me anymore

Are you listening to me

I wasn't supposed to hear how
the cops found your chest collapsed
a steering wheel inside it
and that you tried to tell them something
didn't you?

You—a Hercules, a giant—
head held like a baby
inside a smoldering heap
and by a stranger
all of your efforts for nothing
thick black clot
from your mouth like
the unclogging
of a sewer pipe

Was that a message for me?

You know I used to sit
on the toilet and wonder if
you saw me masturbating
looking in my head
feeling my thoughts
I was so sorry
to keep disappointing you

Then I would pray—
ask in faith and it
will be given—
that when I left the bathroom
when I had cummed
that I would find you
on the couch alive

I didn't have enough faith
to bring you back
and I'm sorry

This is the last of it

Don't expect much more
no matter what I've forgotten

I hope you can understand
I can't keep it up
People are tired of it
I'm tired of it

V.

I'm sorry I can't fix a car like you
I'm sorry I'm not strong
I'm sorry I'm not the son you were
greasy and in Dad's footsteps

I'm sorry I smoke pot
I'm sorry I suck cock
I'm sorry there's no room left
for anything but anger

I'm sorry I stopped w/ that Bible bullshit
I'm sorry for all the things I've thought—
You should see how I
back away from a fight

I'm fucking weak!
I'm fucking spineless!
I can't keep a job
I can't keep a woman

I can't keep this poem to myself
I'm sorry I fucked up your Beach Boys 8 track
I'm sorry I pissed my pants in fourth grade
and you had to drive me home

I'm sorry I touched your cold dead body
I'm sorry that no matter how many poems
I write none of them have the magic

none of them have the power to bring you back

I can't get you out of my head
I can't pray anymore
I'm sorry I didn't stop you
I should have

Time is a circle
we're not even sure it exists
I'm sorry I fucked an Air Force man
in the ass last night

I'm sorry I drink so much
I'm sorry I can't talk to you
and that I hate you for it
I'm sorry I won't visit the tomb

I'm sorry I can't bring myself
to say your name or to whisper
it or share it w/ my friends
I'm sorry this poem can't spare us

all we lose in Leadwood, Missouri
Richie, I'm so sorry
I've written of this before
and made it a mockery.

The Incredible Hulk Goes Grocery Shopping After Taking a Handful of Klonopin

Does Hulk want to smash
Hulk don't know
Hulk just know
the old guy in front of him
is catching up on war stories
w/ this other old guy
right in front of the spicy
pickles Hulk want

Hulk's wife no care
if Hulk gets his goddamn pickles or not
she's just ready to get home

Hulk takes a deep breath
he gets this way sometimes
full of gamma rays, all fists and
unable to speak, but
Hulk's gotten used to
never getting his pickles

Because there's always two
old men standing right in
front of them catching up
on war stories
how's this for a war story:

Try being Bruce Banner
and see if anyone gives
a rat's ass about how
sorry you are for all
the shit you smashed
while green.

Hulk Meets Moloch

and can do nothing but stare in wonder
at the magnificent power of something
so malevolent

Betty wants to buy a house
in the suburbs

Bruce doesn't care as long
as it's close to his lab

But Hulk wants a simpler life
something away from the American
flags and Trump signs
but he's so big
what apartment
would fit him

What god of mercy
would allow him this

He knows his mind isn't right

There are no jobs for him
none that he would take anyway
split personality, you say?

Hulk never corrects them

Why don't you go back to smashing?
You're good at it

Hulk gets so tired of smashing
and w/ Betty's help

he's been working on his pronunciation

He doesn't want to be this anymore
he doesn't want to smash brains
across concrete and aluminum

Still he knows his mind isn't right
and neither is Banner's
and sometimes he even worries
about Betty w/ her father
bent on death

W/ the tanks and guns
W/ the military complex
a burning hatred of Hulk
Hulks wonders if he's America
or if he's the things America hates
Bisexual, mentally ill, so used to night
he feels swaddled in a blanket of darkness

In some ways, though, he
knows he's better off than Bruce
who has to worry about the long term
when Hulk doesn't

Bruce wonders what will happen
if he has to go back into the hospital
check himself in through the ER

Suicidal, homicidal, delusional

nervous, Bruce gets so goddamned
nervous.

The Incredible Hulk Tries to Write a Poem

but his cucumber fingers
keep getting in the way

He smashed the keyboard
all to hell and pencils
mean broken lead and splinters

Pens make a mess that nobody
wants to clean up
Hulk is used to it
he's made so many messes

There's that boy he kissed
and then turned away
there was a woman before Betty
who got tired
of dishes thrown against the wall
and Bruce's wails of agony.
It's just too much, she said

Hulk has so much he wants to say
it lives and breathes inside his green skin
where it will stay for what might
as well be eternity

He wants to write a love poem for Betty Ross
he wants to write 1,000 poems of apology
for Betty and all the rest left in the wake of his anger

If he could just write his way out of this
entire mess, untangle this knot
maybe they would forgive him, he thinks

But Bruce knows forgiveness isn't
given easily and if it comes
it's not going to be the result
of a goddamn poem

Forgiveness comes through silence
or doesn't come at all.

Bruce Banner Wakes Up Hungover

and wonders what Hulk
has done now

Was it a night out w/ women
was it a fist fight in a parking lot
was it case after case of Natural Light

Bruce can't remember
and he's better off that way
he thinks. He's never been
good w/ guilt

It's a river he doesn't
swim well
like he's always
fighting against the current
like the drugs he takes to try
and keep Hulk away

But there's always a Hulk
and there's always a hangover.

Bruce Banner's Intrusive Thoughts

For this poem we have to pretend
that Bruce Banner has a daughter
and that Bruce Banner isn't me

We'll have to pretend that the basement
I write in is his lab

Okay?

Bruce had a fight w/ Betty
Bruce's anxiety was out of control
Bruce's OCD was even worse
Bruce's OCD manifests itself
as intrusive thoughts
he can't help but articulate out loud
Bruce is about to have his dog put down
just like me
Bruce's dog is going to die
just like mine

Bruce paces the lab
he says, *I'm*
going to die today
Bruce says it several times
his daughter overhears

She calls Betty.
Dad is saying scary things
I think you should come home

Dad is saying scary things
Dad is having scary thoughts
Betty, who we must pretend isn't

my wife
tells her daughter it's nothing to worry
about. It's his anxiety

No one knows if it's something to
worry about or not. But it's what
we tell ourselves. It's what we tell
our daughter.

Bruce, Betty and Hulk Figure It All Out

Let them call Bruce what
they want

If he's a cuck
then he's a cuck

But he knows something
the alt right trolls don't
and he didn't find it in a textbook

There are many ways to love
and be in love w/ a woman

Hulk is what he is
Gamma rays
an urge inside of Bruce
he's tired of fighting

They both want to give Betty
a voice in all of this—whether
poetry or science or both

Bruce wants to put on Betty's
lacy nightgown and feel
Hulk inside of his body
instead of his mind
these are thoughts he once
kept to himself, but he knows
there's something inside him
that can't be controlled

And he's finally able to admit
he loves being out of control.

Dawn

She said *where's the receipts*
I said *you're soaking in them*

She said *how much did you spend.*
I said *I squeezed the Charmin, baby*

Not good
Mr. Whipple ain't fucking around

She said *Dan, I'm serious now*
I said *Dan ain't in this poem.*

Paper Anniversary

Somewhere along time
the first year became
the paper anniversary
and we should somehow
write our words on that
as if parched, pressed
tree bark
could hold them

Seems to me we
started our writing
on the wind
drew our words
w/ invisible clarity
to be scattered like leaves
through barren lands
and blue-green fields

Then we wet our fingertips
a little
spelling them out in cursive
on river ripples
erased almost as soon
as we whispered them
and on tidal waves' foam
coming near, moving away

Then, like artists
we etched them out
into soft red clay
put work into our hands
molded them the color
of our bruises

then carried them inside
and called it home

Finally
we carved
our words in stone
letter by letter
a fragment
at a time
we wrote them
I love you.

Sestina McRib

When god pulled that bow of bone
from Adam he couldn't have seen this
coming. Or maybe he could. They say he
sees everything coming. I don't
At least not until it's too late
And now the McRib

is back. Two dollars. It's not really a rib
that's the fast one. This boneless
gift used to be sloppy, out of control. Lately
its act has come together. This
fist full of little problems. I don't
want to sound sentimental, but Ronald, he

must have wept, how he
must have wailed when the McRib
was torn from his side. Lonely doesn't
touch the lack of it. The missing bone
so long a part of his flesh. *This*
you said, sauce on your hands, *isn't real meat* and later

that half-eaten sandwich tempts me. It's late
you are asleep, I am drunk, he
God, not Ronald, would deny me this
I eat anyway, devour it, the McRib,
and the bone
bleached gaze of the moon doesn't

make me feel guilty at all. I do not
feel guilty at all. It's too late
for that. And of Adam, and his lost bone
I wonder if he
missed it? Reached for it at night like

the rib was there only to find this:

                                  this
empty pillow, this car full of empty wrappers. Don't
dwell on it much. Think of the McRib
Even now when it is getting late
try not to think of the way he
must have felt, a sack of meat and missing bones

I saw this coming
too late. Don't
let its lack
of bones fool you
Everything is falling apart
except the McRib.

The Night I Met Larry Brown

The night I met Larry Brown
the catfish weren't biting
He sat down on the barstool
next to me and said *hello
I'm Larry Brown*

He shook his head real slow then.
No, he says, *I'm not. That's a
lie. I'm Richard. I was Larry
Brown's best friend*

The night I met Larry Brown
he had wet brain. He was 32

The night I met Larry Brown
it had all just about gone to hell.
He grabbed the front of my shirt
curled it into his fist.
Larry used to throw dog food
out onto the lake—
Wait, he said. *That story's
not interesting. By the way,
I'm Richard*

The night I met Larry Brown
I thought about how
it all scattered like black birds—
the same ones that flutter
in my chest when I have
the shakes

The night I met Larry Brown
I was in love

The night I met Larry Brown
was the closest I'd come
to a fight in years. But I looked
at myself, grown fat in the
bar room mirror and thought
better of it

The night I met Larry Brown
you better believe I was tired
of being the fat friend

The night I met Larry Brown
he reintroduced himself to me
as Richard seven or eight times
Each time, my shirt, clutched in
his hand

The girl next to me says
she has to quit drinking.
It kills her system.
I tell her that's the point.
Larry Brown agrees

Larry Brown thinks whiskey
is a wonder drug, but
pharmaceutical companies have conspired
to keep it from us. *It gives
your insides a healthy workout*, he says

The night I met Larry Brown
I'm in love

The night I met Larry Brown
he tells me all he ever wanted
was to teach high-school. *I have
what it takes*, he says. *I'm Richard*

His rat faced friend puts his
arm around my shoulder.
Don't mind him, he says
he just gets like this

Like what I say
Drunk he says

The night I met Larry Brown
he asked me what the fuck
it is exactly that I'm trying to be

I didn't have an answer for him.

The night I met Larry Brown
I'm in love w/ either the ghost
of what I should have become
or the joke of what I have

And then somewhere
there's a daughter as blue
as any sky has ever been
as blue as the last note
of this Hank Williams song
as blue as I am
and churning as violently

I couldn't help wonder
what would become of her,
the night I met Larry Brown.

How Me and Lord Byron Got our Grooves Back

I'm having beers
w/ Warren Zevon
we're talking
about our cancers

It's boring
I may not even have
cancer
Warren certainly doesn't

He wants
to invite Kerouac
but I'm tired
and Kerouac
cries into his whiskey
and it always ends when he
demands to be draped in
an American flag and buried
up north

I was tired of everything
at that point
in the deep south
so many miles from my wife
and Adrienne Rich rebuffing
my every advance

Let me show you how it's done
Byron says
I don't know where he came
from but his entrance a
dramatic flapping of a cape
was something to behold

What else can I do
I sit back and watch
It's impressive

You'd think
him a young David Lee Roth
In the end, however
it doesn't go any better
for him that it did me

Tonight, Adrienne says
no poetry will serve
and that seems to be the gist
of the whole goddamned thing

All of us brooding on the mistakes
we just can't seem to write our way
out of
those long-haul problems
stretch out like the Mississippi
waters the deep troubled waters
the anxieties of speaking

The things hidden so well
no one can fault you for them
clasped so tightly no one would
bother to steal them and even if
they did what could they do

We find some joy in that
and a few other things
and think maybe we should
invite old Jack over after all

He may have cried, just a little
trying to compare Byron's cape

to the spasm of a dying catfish

He never did get
that image just right
but Jesus Christ
his hair was.

Threw My I Ching

I throw some pennies
onto the bar

You look them over
for a long time

Finally you draw lines
onto a piece of paper
and say *this is the wind*

Very well, I am the wind

I move through the South
a whisper

You say
it means a change is coming

As if those broken
homes in Missouri
mean a thing

All of this, I know, is bullshit

I'd not had a drink in four days
until I laid those pennies down

So which course do I take?
I throw again

You call it thunder
and this I know well
thunder keeps me silent

I spend my days drinking thunder away

It's violent, loud
alcohol shuts my thunder mouth

I shrug it off
we move on to the next bar

And throw again
you always look
better under neon

This one, you say
is the mountain

This is the me I kill every night.

Stigmata

        You say the stigmata is a fake
I say *dear* and want to argue but
outside, in the dark, something calls to me
        the virgin mother, the moon, a chipmunk
and I wonder if the stigmata has come
or if a bleeding ulcer might count
as walking in Jesus' footsteps

Later, when I try to fall asleep
alone on the couch, I will read
        cover enquirer: stigmata signs
autographs in blood, snapshots a wound

They made a movie—the direction
cut to a painting of Jesus Christ
cue scary music, close up of hands
he is always forlorn in these things
        head heavy w/ thorns
the stigmata needs a hug

I found mine in a box at the gas station
        FREE
I brought it home, laid down newspaper
smacked its nose when it bled on the floor
        fed it table scraps, patted its head
until my wife made me get rid of it

I had no choice, what could I do then
but put it in a sack, drive it out
to the country and let it go
as it ran off it made connections
between earth and everyday things
looking over its shoulder at me

tail between its legs, I think it cried
        one red tear down a cherubic cheek

Now the stigmata has come farther
than me, Sesame Street and all those
ragged, holy, Reaganomic boys
it pulled out of this town and made it
        now shout it to the rooftops, sister
now say it w/ me again, my wife
now let it bring you back, my brother

It is a glorious thing to bleed
it is a glorious thing to clean
though it is not for everyone

There's a drop of rain on my window
there're headlights backing down the drive
there's Morse code in everything
symbols that we take for granted
        but the drum of this rain is easy

I see it on the face of the old
woman behind the bar, and on the
kneecap of a boy, pressed like a rose
        turned to dust between the pages
of our photo album.

I Wish My Wife Liked Me Half as Much as She Likes *Fargo*

We ride in silence
she's not speaking to me
and there's no song on the radio
sad enough to do any of it justice

But when we get to our
friend's house and he turns on
Fargo she laughs like the hinges
have fallen from the gates

Maybe it has something
to do w/ our years
in those cold Michigan
winters

The Decembers where
I did such bad things
no one could ever really
get over them

She tries to forgive
claims she has
but no one ever forgives
and Jesus died for shit

Or maybe she just
likes the show.
I'll need beer later.
Slow killing

She's a good wife
known to use my mental illness

against me
but what sane person hasn't?

And she usually catches herself
apologizes for something I didn't
even notice because I'm watching
the night sky as we drive home

Fargo was good tonight
I say
Sure
she says.

I Used to Be Someone's Favorite Eclipse

Before
the real darkness came
like a long, labored wink

Before the dragon ate the sun
I used to be someone's favorite
tragedy

Then the real darkness came

I see it in my cup of morning coffee
I see it in my pupil
I feel it burrowing holes
into me

I'm paranoid again
on the downside of mania

I hear it in her voice
when she asks if I
can just please
get out of bed

Before the real darkness came
I used to be someone's favorite
burning sun
brighter than first love
brighter than a single fish
scale alone on a dock

I won't let it worry me
it'll pass until the sky aligns just right
again, even then

My wife never got that beautiful
diamond ring she wanted, but
in consolation

my pills look like white moons.

If I was Magic

Watching you as you slept
        I wondered if you'd ever done the same
You were alien to me
        everything you'd ever told me false

        We bought Drano today
the sink has gone slowly
        we found it on sale
the tidy things
the tidy sink
below tidy cabinets
where tidy medications await tidy hands
        and mouths

You made sunflower curtains
from your old dress
to hang in the room
you'd given me to be alone in
        I covered the windows w/ them

I watch you as you sleep
        breath seamless
even as stitch
there is not enough yelling in our house
        especially at midnight

to be a sorcerer
        toss bones to the floor
what is to be seen in those things
        words cannot conjure
the scary face of contentment

your lover voice

to your wife voice
to your mother voice

my days chew cud

the goddamn winter in Michigan has begun

if I would have written this when I was younger
I'd know how to end it now

I'd fall so close to something
that I couldn't see it anymore

I'd stop watching you
          my chest rising and falling
in tune w/ your back.

I Married a Sling Blade

We're watching Sling Blade
and I'm laughing my ass off
Margaret says *I don't think
it's supposed to be so funny*

Doyle pushes some dude in a wheelchair
into the wall and he splays
like a crash test dummy
                              dot dot dot like the poets do

It's not funny Margaret says

That Frank, he lives inside of his own heart

Holy Christ I say
one minute Karl doesn't know
where he is
the next he's spouting poetry

That's you Margaret says
I married a fucking Sling Blade

Then we're both laughing
but later I think
maybe she's right
She works in mental health
after all

As did I for a year
and all I remember:

            There was Carol who spoke to the Raspberry Spirits.

There was Mike who showed me the peppermint god
breaking through the violent clouds like a fist.

There was Joe who thought he was Jesus and spit
in my face as a blessing. When he tried to stab me
w/ a pencil I grabbed his wrist. It was as soft as a
petal and as delicate as a pistil.

There was Leigh the Magdalene who wouldn't shit.
We held her down, someone, possibly me, had
to stick his finger into the dark spider hole of her
ass to see if she was impacted and maybe I imagined
myself going through a tunnel like a death vision
and speaking in tongues from her mouth, a ghost.

There was Teresa, who Marvin, close to retiring,
headbutted when she refused her meds. I kissed
the wound and left w/ bloody lips.

Well, if I'm a Sling Blade
I guess I'm a Sling Blade
I laugh at all the things that
aren't funny. Like the dead
poets. The dead relatives. All the
goddamned lead.

> Leigh said *Jesus doesn't want me to have a bowel*
> *movement. He hates filth*
> Shh I said, stroking her long gray hair. *It's the filth*
> *he loves the most*

If I could do the voice
The Sling Blade voice
the beautiful things I would say
But eventually, it has to stop, right
the saying of all these things?

C is for Cookie

I won't believe this is real
anymore. Like I'm going to just
lay here all night shaking, thinking again
of the cookie when there is a jar full
in the kitchen and if those are gone
a gas station just down the road

It's hard. My father loved the Oreo
and his father the macaroon. It was
good enough for them, I thought
it's good enough for me

But cookies are what got me into this
mess, cookies are why I quiver
but I'd known only hunger when
the chickens from my cookie eating
days finally came home to roost

The things I did all hopped up
on cookies do not suffer forgiveness

I've been a bad monster. In my endless
thirst maybe

I wasn't thinking straight. Maybe
she'd just given me all the forgiveness
she had to give. Maybe it didn't matter
that I had given up cookies
because I still thought of them. I still
kept one in my desk drawer just in case

You don't have to talk when you've got
a fig newton in your mouth. There's no

room to think w/ a mind full of sugar

So when she asked
I cracked one wide
and a million different
fortunes spread before us

I opened my mouth to
say so but it hung
a gaping black wound

all my life I've known silence
except deep down
where it whispers
insistently
madly
finally

Cookie
Cookie
Cookie!

Ashley's Poem

I.

Before you were born
your mother and I, drunk, dissolved
into our dreams
too in love to handle reality we wrote
in tiny circles, in clichés
so small they fit into the pink of your hand

Then somewhere along that line we changed
freed ourselves from drying mud
and the poets
didn't seem as important anymore
and you
growing already somewhere deep and dark
a secret place I'd visit
stumbling my own way through hell

Today, I look at your hands and see my hands
I look in your eyes and see my eyes
I whisper and wonder if you understand
your mother was never held in a father's arms like this

One second old
I held you
already time taunts you and falls out of sight
one breath becomes one million

Your father's got a case of the shakes.

II.

The nurses divide us w/ paper walls
the woman on the other side
another new mother speaks on the phone
Have you given any thoughts as to what we'll name it?

A boy, small as an aspirin
compared to you
his brittleness cupped by a dead-faced mother

She tells us, she tells the nurse, she tells anyone who will listen
His daddy better get here soon if he wants to name him
already the boy is two days old
and knows only the fake
burnt-out smiles of nurses
and the empty glare of his mother

She holds her baby
like he is a rat
as no one continues to visit them

Your family walks past her
because everyone that visits this room
comes for you

I want to grab that no-name boy
I'm your father I'll say
and this is what it's like to be held in strong arms
this is the smell of aftershave
and this is the feel of stubble on a chin
grown old

I will name you
I will name you Messiah.

III.

Ashley,
You've already fooled me
into believing, again, that youth lasts forever

They took a picture of us today
and someday, when you're angry w/ me
because I don't know what life is like
I will show you this picture
and I will say *look*
that was your daddy
he was a black-haired, handsome man

Your mother thin and alive w/ you

And I will show you this poem
and ask you to remember that nameless tiny boy

When I no longer can

I will ask you
where is the young man that shared a room w/ you

The one who breathed the first air that you breathed

He is your brother
now name him.

The Unclean

Abomination

the night the earth howled
in birth
stopped
at the very fiery core
of pregnancy
I was alone

and the fire poured
from the sky
in long tongues
of

Jeffry itched
a scab
an open wound
a pustule
or blotch

he was getting thin by then

the earth howled
I said
and twisted metal smoked
lord he was getting thin

and the flames roared
and the smoke ran like rivers of blood
chasing screams through the streets
where they were lost
in glass jars

momma used to stack
end on end
like bricks
full of pig's feet
eggs
brain of lamb
pickled in brine

and dear god was my boy thin

it was 1982
and the earth howled
holocaust

it was 2001
and the earth howled
war

and dear god
there was death in the air.

Gemini

My lover comes to me
hands me a drink
whiskey and coke

her hands cold and wet
from beads of sweat
dead on the glass

she smiles and I'm lost somewhere
and I'm not exactly sure
how to get back
but it has something to do w/ a road
and a light

how are you feeling
on tv the world is ending
again

you need to flick your ash
on tv the wagons circle around a camp fire
it's winter
and the cowboys are soaking
blankets in death

you're going to burn yourself
on tv no man stands alone
and all I can think of
is what to wear to the bar tonight
I like to be watched
the hungry gaze of men
lust dripping from their mouths
like cancer on leather

there's a sense of power
in the tight body
of youth

have you eaten today
on tv my ash falls to the floor
a still smoldering cherry
eats into the carpet
and it smells somewhere between
burning hair and boiling flesh.

Abomination

     Jeffry the powder
     isn't working

         what are you talking about

     the powder isn't working
     I can still see them

           even from there

sucking wounds

Jeffry cries
he lost his job today
it's 1982
his dick hasn't been hard in months
and his asshole is raw from wiping

bring me a male w/out blemish
he says
and tries to laugh

pray w/ me
he asks

I light a cigarette
his dick hasn't been hard in months
on the television
there is a gnashing of teeth
Jeffry touches my cheek
his flesh on fire
it's the new cancer

and Jerry Falwell

    gawd hath unlaid
    his protective hand
    from Sodom

the television

    I said gawd
    hath unlaid
    his protective hand
    from a modern day
    Sodom

he hath unlaid
his hand you see
and hell hath
broken forth
through fertile earth
through concrete
through glass
through steel

and gawd hath unlaid
his protective hand

dear gawd, son, you are thin
and our lord hath unlaid
his protective hand
can't you see

and I have come across a vision
and it has been revealed unto me
that your dick has not been hard in months
and that your ass is hamburger meat
sizzling blood oozes

you see, boy, gawd hath unlaid
his protective hand
can you hear the snap of grease
that is fire, son
fire.

Gemini

My mother used to
fix me hamburgers
two at a time
after a double shift
her eyes tired
were clots
she had nothing else for me

two hamburgers
every night religiously
no matter what
I had fixed myself for supper
I ate them
it was better than rabbit or squirrel
which I had also eaten
and which my grandmother had
cast as unclean

two hamburgers
a diet Coke
it wasn't until I'd
learned the good use
of my two front fingers
that I learned thin

are you ok
i wake up to static
the lingering smell of
my mother's neck
makes me hungry

and I lay my wife down
dick hard

fucking away
whatever it was
I'd seen on the television
sparkling on the television
before sleep

and I'm burning
here
in this hole that is soft and wet and on fire
and somewhere inside
Mr. Bones is lost

                      and he isn't sure how to get back
but it has something to do w/ a light and a road.

River

They took us down there as kids
and showed us where the dead bodies were found
a boy and a girl
decapitated and genitals mangled
somewhere between the ages of 14 and 17
no one could tell for sure
but Chad swore
he could still see stains of blood
baked into the rock

this was in April
and still it was cold
and the mono-myth
just wasn't working anymore

this was after I'd sucked Chad off
and he'd convinced himself
we were still sane
'cause we were young
and we were cousins

      there's a panther in a zoo in a cage

and sometimes I can still taste him
thick as hamburger
      and at church the smell of rotten
apples clung to the linen
      draped red at the altar

what do we do when the metaphors fail
and the analogies beg us to leave them alone
and all those dead Greeks are dead for good

momma my boy is thin
his sores are like mouths
his dick hasn't been hard in months
and his ass is raw hamburger meat

and there's this guy on television
you see

and the earth is howling
struck blind and dumb
by some fool on television

and the blood's still in the river
Chad's there as well
his dick hard and his mind sane
       and there's a panther in a cage
       and there's lamb brains in a jar
dear god
I'd only gone down to the river

and the faceless dead
marched like wraiths out of the waters
away from the shores
and into the city to burn.

The City

I have a friend
who writes me from there
I'm going to show him how to hunt
the power of a lithe body
in blue jeans
somewhere in Missouri
where they continue to dance
chewing their lips
it's 1960
and the draft
has called him up

he had a brother in 'Nam
who let him die
who let him die
who could have saved him
and who let him die
he had a brother in 'Nam
who let him die

there's a dead man on the television
who has let him die
fuck metaphor
Ronald Reagan is on television
and he has let his brothers die.

Gemini

Was baptized
7 or 8 times
as a kid
it never stuck

oh death
there is a war a ragin'
oh death
there is a war

I was groomed
as the next family preacher

oh death
where the lilacs had fallen
where the oil had spilt
oh death

Jeffry isn't coming home
and his touch won't find me
and the healing we'd prayed for
just won't come.

Missouri

Dave and I walk into a bar
insert your own punch line here
the second guy ducked
the bartender said *but you're a gorilla*
the priest eats nun on Fridays
after he's flossed his teeth w/ cock
you fuck her
to get to the other side
it stands for *got aids yet*
and the other guy said
I didn't know it was a smorgasbord
yippee eye aye cowboy
cowboy

and the old guy at the bar
he says
yep, the old guy at the bar says
underneath his straw hat
he could have been my father
and he says
to his friends
he only has two teeth, you see
two rotten teeth
two black buck teeth
charred in smoke
and he says
he says to his buddies
blacks (but he doesn't say blacks) *and faggots fellas*
blacks and faggots
this town's bein' overrun
by (blank) *and* (blank)

and the other guy says

    my god it's burning up in here
I'm burning up
   it feels like my blood is boiling
turn off the tv and pray w/ me
   my cock hasn't been hard in months
my wounds won't heal
   and my ass is dripping mad cow disease
and he says *kiss me*
   are you afraid
   are my lips that scary
I was having this
it's hot in here
   I remember my little brother
before he drowned
and this red ball he had
and how we used to bounce it
and dear god I was only going there to pray
outside next to the pool
and the cowboy says
no thanks, ma'am
back home we like
the girls who sing soprano
   you shall not eat that which is unclean
   you should have seen how he laughed
when I'd pretend that balloon was something too big for me
that its weight had crushed me to the earth

did you ever eat squirrel I asked
no he answered
it taste like the dark meat of chicken
after it's been left on
the counter a few days
sounds yummy he said
he would try to make me
laugh like that sometimes
even after the disease had

taken the better part of him
he'd take his limp lesioned dick and make it talk
    Death to Republicans
it would say
and he says
and gawd hath unlaid his hand.

Family

It's 1957
my father is 16 years old
the earth has stopped to howl
god is dead
and dad's dropped out of school
to take care of my great-grandmother

he is not yet married
but flesh isn't new to him
his son has yet to die
America is strong
and a man needs nothing
but strong hands
to work

his cock bulges
against a faded blue
silhouette on his jeans
work is good
and the lay-off
won't come until
he's old w/ three children

I used to hunt rabbits w/ a stick
I'd follow their shit balls
and tracks
w/out a gun
I'd break their skulls w/
the stick I'd found
take them home
covered in red snow
for momma
to skin and fry

a few stray rabbit hairs
popping maniacally in grease

it's like chicken
really cute chicken
that you'd broken open
w/ a stick

and I wondered
what was going into the jar

dad's nine years old
and he's at the river
there's a boy w/ him
and they'd never before kissed

their poles bending
under the moon
half-full and red
just above Venus.

Halloween

A girl at school shows my daughter a newspaper
that reads *Invisible Killer Loose in America*
she doesn't want to trick or treat this year
there's death in the air
decay in October
and my wife says *you never know*
what someone might put in the candy
and the television says
and the guy I've been having cyber-sex w/ says
stay away from the malls

there's a silent killer loose in America
I'd seen him
a shadow in the woods
when I was a boy
and I'd went down to the river to pray

they never found out who did it
but I had an idea
he was wearing a Reagan mask
or something
and he was somebody's father
I'd seen when I was sleeping
and there was a crash
and the flames ate god
and the river was low
w/ drought.

Gemini

My father is dead
and my father's father
and my lover's smoking
Marlboro Lights in the next room
w/ the television on
the flames are eating god
      you see
you can turn down the volume
but the screams still come
      you see
            my dick hasn't been hard in months
            snot is flowing a river from my nose
            my eyes are the color of death
            and dear god when did I get so thin.

City

Nobody's coming back
they were lost
drowned in flame
that won't rise again

they were brave
it is always brave to die
just ask them
you can hear them on the wind
through the trees
and on the dark undercurrent
of the river.

River

I stopped to pick up a stone
smooth in my hand as flesh
damp and cool
it's where my father was found
I'd went to see the bodies
but they were gone
washed away
in dark waves of plastic
Timmy said:
        they cut their stuff up, man
        cut that guy's dick up and that girl's pussy out
        left nothin' but black holes of nothin'
        you could see up in 'em, man
        and it was black
        it was black and guts and stink.

Father

My father had fished there as a child
and his father had left him w/out a word
and never returned
of course you couldn't eat anything out of there now
too much junk in the water
but he'd stopped his family from going hungry more than once
there before the meth and the needles and the knowing of lead

the last time I saw him
he was surrounded by flowers
his face was swollen as a catcher's mitt
his hair smelled of ash
his hands looked as if they'd been soaked in brine
his wedding ring was missing
        but this was just in a dream I'd seen on television
dear god
        this was just a dream
dear god
        I only saw it in a dream

he called me yesterday
I wasn't home
and he didn't leave a message
but I can recognize his silence anywhere.

Jeffry

could hardly speak
his eye sight gone
and all I wanted to do was touch him
but I was afraid
even his own mother was afraid
there were these people on television
it was 1984 and god was killing faggots
one red blood cell at a time
and Jeffry had turned brown
like a fern in a fire
one white blood cell at a time
I'd gone hysterical
he'd gone blank
        kiss me kiss me kiss me   kiss me   kiss me
I can't I just fuckin' can't all right
it was all I could do to keep from throwing him into the
goddamned river

it was an abomination
Frankenstein's monster
the leper
on television
Milton Berle in drag
his wrist limp
it's hilarious
the audience can't control themselves.

The River

My father had cut the throat
of his first deer there
the blood had spilled out onto the rock
he'd gutted it
from neck to nuts
and threw the intestines into the river
where they floated away
becoming part of the great nothing
he'd left the coat and head and testicles for the flies
they laid their babies in the soft down of its eyes
until the maggots burst from eyes to nose to mouth
the meat was taken home and eaten.

Halloween

I'd spent my first halloween as a dead deer
and last night we had a party
my house full of masks and strange scents
my wife had come as chrysanthemums
most had come as demons
or fun-house mirrors
and there I was
the flame of a candle
reflected a thousand thousand times

Jeffry had come as a skeleton
six years after he had died
my father had come as a hunter
my mother had disappeared somewhere
in the pop of hamburger grease
and I knelt down to pray
      jesus
        dear jesus
gawd hath unlaid his protective hand
      I'd only gone to the river to pray *oh death*
gawd hath struck w/ fire
      brothers
gawd hath smited and laughed
      I'd only
gawd
      went down
gawd
      went down
gawd
      jesus
gawd
      to the river to pray

I was seven years old
my brother had a red ball
I'd been across the street w/ Timmy Conway
we'd found a dead snake
its scales
had grown brown in the heat of the sun
oh death
we picked at its insides w/ sticks
my father had been down at the river
looking for my cousin and me
    you boys better not be doing what I think you're doing
his dick hadn't been hard in months
my mother was making hamburgers
she'd burnt her wrist w/ grease
and dear god her boy was thin.

How Many Miles Must I Run before I Beat Depression

Because sane people keep
telling me it will help
they write article after
article about it
and publish them in places
sane people read
like Salon

Can I just kick my legs
in bed like my dog dreaming
he seems happy enough

But they say it has something
to do w/ the sun
feeling your feet hit pavement
making contact w/ the physical world

I hate to rain on it, sane people
but my sister died of melanoma
how the fuck you like the sun now

I'm sure you like it just fine
you like everything just fine
like super fruits
or that herb you just heard about

Look, I'm not getting out of bed today

When I'm manic
I don't need your advice
when I'm depressed
I won't take it

Choke on your pomegranate
I have this poem
and I've written it until
my feet are blistered and bloody.

South 55

It's like it always is
everything looks the same
especially in Arkansas

She said she'd follow me to
hell, but through this land
where everything is yellow

This is mud
This is dead country
This is a wife pregnant w/ spiders

You call and
ask where I'm at
Memphis
I once laid a red-headed
bartender at the Peabody
but I don't tell you that

It was good

Coming from Nashville
you want to meet at
such and such an exit

and like always
I do

You touch my hand
at the Waffle House
before handing me
my ticket
your mouth is dry

a crushed diamond

I know your skin
the spiral of
freckles on your left shoulder

If it killed me
I didn't notice

You want me to follow you home
but I'm not going home

I can see you smiling
in mirrored glasses
several states behind me

If I can't think of
anything pretty to say
about it
I'm sorry

and two days later
we're lying in bed
me and Mississippi
too afraid to touch
we open the window
watch the thunder storm
until the whole damn state
falls asleep
I listen to the breathing
thunder
your breathing
the awning outside
looks like a bear
in the dark

If it killed
I've always been
a miracle at forgetting

even in this dark country
even in this year of cancer
even w/ all of this
I come back, Mississippi.

Some Fava Beans

Years of heavy drinking
finally caught up w/ me
so I went to my doctor
for one of those new livers

He had a nice healthy one
in a jar on his desk
I'd had my eye on it for months

Gimme that liver I said

Sorry he said, *that liver's taken*

I couldn't believe it

> Yep, son, that liver there
> belongs to Mickey Mantle
> I don't mind telling you
> I'm a pretty big fan

Mickey goddamned Mantle

He's got to be at least 110, man

Oh, he's been dead for years
the doctor said
I've got two kids
I need that good, brown liver

*Maybe you shouldn't drink so much
then* the doctor said

Me? What about Mickey

goddamned Mantle?

Nothing I can do the doctor said
    I've got a nice spleen out back
    if you want it, a couple of kidneys
    I could make a deal on

but this liver is going
to The Mick

        He's a national treasure
        He married a model
        He's been to the White House
        seven or eight times
        What have you done?

I'm a poet I say

        Kid, get the hell out
        of my office. And do us
        both a favor, don't
        come back.

Eat

At Schnucks a lean woman
puts low-fat butter into her cart
then at Wal-Mart a man
sneaks diet pills into his coat pocket
later, at Denny's, I watch old folks
order from the "Fit Fare" menu

My wife looks me over before she finally says
maybe you should try something low carb

To this I say *no*
I will eat

I will eat w/ abandon and love it
as none have loved it before me
fat will hang from my bones
in great folds. Shake like
blinds in a gale when I laugh

My fat will be an avalanche

I will wear the greasy lips of a hamburger
eating man. I'll wipe my Cheeto-stained hands
upon my sweat pants and not give a damn who's watching

When I hit 1000 pounds, I'll make the talk show circuit

*Well, Ellen, I don't really have any regrets. I'm a man of
many vices and all in all it's been a pretty good life.* Ellen
won't believe me of course, but then again
she has to stay thin for television

When I die, my children will have a hard time finding

a casket for me

They'll have to bust the church door
down off its hinges to fit me in. When they sing "How
Great
Thou Art"
they'll be talking about Taco Bell

When people ask my wife *what happened*
the smile of gorged passion still wet
upon my lips will be her answer.

The Berryman Thud *(A Dramatic Monologue)*

You ever worry about that guy
from the Oak Ridge Boys
you know, the one w/ the giant
beard

Certainly by now he wishes
he could shave it off
one stupid decision made
in his early twenties he
can't escape

because it's just not the
real Oak Ridge Boys
experience w/out that beard

Well, I worry
about it, man

All that itching
the maintenance
the shampooing
alone must take forever

You know, I saw them in concert once
his dead eyes still haunt me
since then, I'll often
lay in bed at night
and think about
Berryman's final
plunge off that bridge
somewhere up North where
the Mississippi River
barely exists

except instead of Berryman
it's the guy from the Oak Ridge Boys
his beard reaches toward the heavens
like it has a soul of its own
he's singing Elvira
he doesn't even hit the water
just mud

From what I can tell
and this is all based on body language
like that guy from O'Reilly does
the other three are doing just fine

Look, in the end
I know it's hard
to feel sorry for a rich
straight white guy
but I do

Especially when I think of him
laying awake in bed at night
overcome w/ grief and
stroking his beard
wondering what the hell
he's done w/ his life.

They Haven't Called It a Complex in Forty Years

My wife thinks I should see
a psychiatrist about it
and leave her the hell alone

So, I do. He has
a list of questions for me
He asks is if I'm
straight or gay

A little bit of both I say

What he asks
like Frank Nelson
(that's a reference for you young folks)

A fat wooden cross covers
half a wall. A Samurai sword hangs
on another

He scribbles
something onto his notepad

I ask if everything
is okay.

Yes, Yessssss he says
*It's just that
this is exciting. I've never
met one before*

One what I want to know
One of you he says
I mean the boy version

He asks about my wife
my job, my kids
but, oddly enough
never about my mother

When he's done
we sit in silence
staring at each other
it would become a habit
of ours

Finally, he asks if I'm depressed
No more than any other poet I say

He doesn't find it
funny

Close your eyes he says
*Breathe deep. Imagine
you're in the final match of a big
karate tournament
This is kind of like that
No time for jokes*

For three years
this guy never made
a metaphor that didn't
have karate in it

He fancied them parables

So he says *what do you
think is wrong w/ you
Frankly* I say *I don't think
it's any of my business*

I guess he tried
it couldn't have been fun
for him either

He really only ever
gave me one piece of advice
At night he said *think about
a lake.* The moon is full
The water gently laps
against the shore
The music of the frogs
and crickets lulls you off to sleep

He had a real way w/ words

Look, I don't know if
he had actually ever been camping
but I know that

I fucking hate lakes
the mud
the leeches
the things that brush
against you beneath
the deep, filthy
water.

The Great British Baking Show

I hear my wife and daughter
laughing in the next room
over something someone
said on a show

I'm alone in my office
working on a poem
nothing in the world
could make me laugh today

It's not me
it's part of the illness
I am the illness

Some days nothing
stops my laughter
it shakes like branches

Today
w/ a blunt instrument
whatever causes one to laugh
has been cut out

It sits at my feet like
a bloody and purring kitten
while the voice of family fades
I slip further and further
away

There's no poetic way
to put this
I'm contemplating suicide

Then
on the television
as far away as a star
in the night, someone cries

because their crust didn't
come out flaky enough

Well, I guess that's
kind of funny.

All Hail Walmart

I like the way your long lines look
from the back, Walmart
Walmart, I love your everyday
low prices
and your bell ringers, Walmart
I'll give tomorrow
Almighty Walmart
Walmart the merciless
quaking beneath the shadow
of Walmart
Buying all the AR-15s growing
in the womb of Walmart
All loving Walmart
Food stamp Walmart
I'm wallowing in depression, Walmart
Walmart your prescription medications
have given me erectile dysfunction
Walmart I wait for days for your prescription
medications
Walmart I like how fast you get them done
I like how you *Git 'er Done*
I like you bloody and beaten a little bit
Walmart
Walmart I'm sorry. It won't happen again
I saw Walt Whitman and Walt Disney in your
pale blue eyes Walmart
Walmart we're full of clichés
Walmart
Walmart the blessed
Hallowed be they name.

Why We Kill Ourselves

Because every day is pain
Because we have to ask our
wives to drive us everywhere
Because we've suddenly developed
driving anxiety
Because most days we have anxiety
Because most days we feel bad
about how our anxiety effects our family
Because we did bad things manic
I don't need to get into them here
We all know what we did
and our wives were none too happy about it
Because we were in bed all day
Because we wonder what our children
think when we're in bed all day
Did I mention the shit we did manic?

Look here
it's because we have these
intrusive thought all day long
Kill yourself. I'm going to kill myself.
I'm going to die today. It's over.

All fucking day

Because our brains happen to be
wired that way
Because our daughters heard
us articulate these thoughts compulsively
Because Berryman did it
Plath did it
All of them and
none of this was ever
a cry for help.

What 'Possums Want You to Believe

We have twice again as many teeth
as Andre the Giant
this was, of course, before
we killed Andre the Giant

We wrote, arranged and produced
Pink Floyd's *The Wall*

When we play 'possum
we're not really playing at all

We don't make good pets

In 1980 we had our own miracle on ice
it was something else
you should have seen it

Our tails are as fun as they look

We're not afraid of anything
but we are, next to the armadillo
the second most suicidal animal
in the world

something about those bright lights
like Gods
that could take us
almost anywhere.

What Spider-Man Dreams Of
With great power comes great responsibility.
—Uncle Ben Parker

Showing up late for work

Sex w/out a condom

Turning off the police scanner
and opening a bottle of Jack

Not returning
The Fantastic Mr. Fox
until Monday

Mary Jane's sister

Telling Wolverine to fuck off

SPIDEYMAN SMASH!

Dropping one, just one, old lady

What's on TV tonight

Wings like the Vulture

Surprisingly, not J. Jonah Jameson

Parking tickets

Swinging out of New York
past the skyscrapers
low into the telephone poles
where all sounds are
the remembrance of sound

until somewhere
in the middle of Nebraska
there's nowhere left
to swing anymore
and no one left to save.

Oscar the Grouch
> *Bitch, I live in a fuckin' trashcan.*
> —Dave Chapelle

It's not so bad really
I don't mind the mess
or the occasional half-eaten
hotdog

I like to rattle around
in my tin can

So Ruthie if you want
to tell me a story
keep Lexapro out of it
I got the straight dope
down here

Out there
beyond this manhole
there's tap dancing and counting
there's Buzz Aldrin and Maya Angelou
fantastic beasts and birds

But down here
in the empty bottles and leaky pipes
talking rats and government cheese
the tinny sound of these great walls
Dear God, could be a rocket.

Mania Makes Me a Better Poet

Although it's taboo to say so
it upsets the sane
we are supposed to say we're stable
we're happy
and we probably are
but we're still missing
a little of the chaos magic
a wind that blows in from nowhere

We're supposed to say we're
better now
and we are
we are

a wind that blows in from nowhere

We take our Vraylar
We take our Latuda
We take our Lithium
and Klonopin
and Valiums

because of the wake of destruction
left in the path of our hurricanes
they don't want us to feel good
just normal

This was going to be an essay
until I didn't take my medications
for three days. Now it's
lumbering on the horizon

It's 3:06 am

I've had Nyquil
and the rest of the
self-medications

so I take notice of this moment
of life

You know your meds are working
when you feel dead inside.

Jazz

I don't like it
I never know when
to clap

I'm supposed to like it
appreciate it
dig it
but words
get buried
bone deep

If Jazz is so goddamned good
why did Jack Kerouac feel
the obsessive need to talk
over it
drink through it

On karaoke night
I walk into the bar
instead of karaoke
it's a fucking jazz band

and the drums
are crazy
a strange and beautiful
ending

I'm alone. I talk
to the bartender
when I can
the only
rhythm in this place is OCD

I don't realize I'm in
the middle of a cliché until an old
man sits next to me

A close-talker
his breath smells
like vomit

The drums are a wicked
rebuke. An apocalyptic
god mouth

I know that doesn't make
sense sometimes
you string a few words together
just to get lost in them

The old guy tells the bartender
a homophobic joke
He meanders. It
takes too long
the punchline is stumbling
home

But when he gets there
it's something about why
you can't put a missing gay
kid's picture on a carton of
milk anymore

Everybody gets offended
by the word homo

And bisexuals he says
you have to put their face
on a carton of half and half

Then I'm thinking half and half
half and half, over and over
like it's complex
I heard half and half and
half

For a moment there's relief
and I remind myself that in
all the billions of years
one could have been alive
1995 was a pretty good one

The drums are
not quite my footsteps
two hours in the future
walking home—
but something like it
something close to it
something that sounds like it
half the beautiful and strange
sound of it

When the bartender walks away
the sax sounds manic and blue
all at once and

I nearly die when all the pretty
people in their nice coats clap

Pukey leans in close
asks if I swing to the right
I don't know what that means
I say

He asks where I come from
When I say Leadwood

he says *well son of a bitch*
me too you son of a bitch

I turn my face away
I can't stand the smell
like a rotting possum
like lead
like my dead dad

All I do is nod and nod and nod

He says *You heard of the committee of 300?*
I nod
He says *How about the Bilderberg group?*
I nod
Six people control everything he says
the Queen of England is one of them
I nod, but
I'm thinking
strange and beautiful
thoughts
like half and half and half and

Then the other thoughts pound
it out
It's not real, I think

My mind has turned on me
I know that
everything is off
the light
the stove
my computer
Jazz wasn't built for alcohol

They want to give me pills

Blame it on the Bilderberg group
I guess
blame it on the half and half
blame it on the rain or neurons that fire
like guns blame it on this motherfucker
or what I'm
going to do tomorrow

I can't stop hearing it

The old man is here still
his breath like vomit
The future is here
it's breath and sound
stumbling home

He's not just homophobic
and racist. He may be insane
or on something

Do I feel sorry for him? Can I?
Can empathy stretch like veins
for miles

If you cut open your arm
pull them free
can they reach the moon just
like JFK said?

I guess so
I guess so

Still, I can't stand the smell
I can't stand the rain
blame it on whatever you want

I pay up. I walk home alone.
My breath is fog, my footsteps
a wavering heart

my thoughts a beat

I'm going to kill myself tomorrow
I'm going to kill myself tomorrow
I'm going to kill myself tomorrow.

Dinged

They say the earth vibrates
a remnant from being dinged
by an asteroid or two before
memory was invented

They say we can't feel it
but I swear to god I can
under foot—ringing
like a plate dropped w/out
breaking in the kitchen

But the world won't
just crack open, will it
won't just open wide, split
will it

I have fears
and enemies everywhere

There's the goddamn email
The Shadow men
The Mandela Effect

All these superstitions
like straightening empty
beer bottles at the bar until
they barely touch
like reluctant lovers

She moves over to turn
them, to make sure the
labels face the same direction

and there they are
a little army

Sometimes you need
a woman who'll help you
straighten bottles

So you can say
I like the way you
straighten them bottles, mama

And sometimes you need
a woman who'll knock them down
kill w/ a fist

But no one can do both, right?
That's something no one can do.

And if they start to fall
that's all right

No one can feel us vibrating

No one knows we're about
to split wide open full
of lava and lice

I mean, as long as we're funny, right?
As long as we say funny things

no one will know we're
about to crack
like an egg full
of spiders

Will they?

You Better Fucking Believe There's a Monster at the End of this Book

So you've written a poem about every
goddamned person on this street but me?
Is that about right?

I know my book was scary, but come on
I tried to warn you. Don't turn the page
There's a monster at the end of this book

Did I look like I was kidding?
But you had to keep going

Well, buddy, I hope you're happy
because there's more. That's right,
turn those pages, asshole

Look here, that's the birth
of Grover's daughter. On page 28
we'll relive Grover's DWI

Page 45? That's my mid-life crisis

Keep going and you'll see my struggle
w/ existentialism. Grover had a hell
of a divorce

The name of the monster at the end
of this book is cancer. It's addiction. It's
page after page of boredom and self-doubt

It's time you stop blaming me
If you could have, even once,
just stopped, practiced even a modicum of

self-control, you
would have never come to that

bulbous nose, those longing eyes,
that blue fur, even now, sprouting
across the compass of your body

You'd never have had to weep at the sounds
of your own wavering voice.

In Response to the Article "10 People to Rid Yourself of before the New Year"

Leave them behind
the wounded, the addicted
the fucked up

The cheaters, the liars
and the mother fuckers

The bastards, the bitches
the mentally ill

The pill poppers, the drunks
the cutters and the out and out
pieces of shit

Give them to me. These
are the people I want

The humans, the disconnected
the holy rollers

All of these beautiful sons
and daughters

Everyone who has given up

I'll take each and every one

It's going to be all right I'll say

Shhh everything
is going to be all right.

Acknowledgments:

Books:

People Everyday and Other Poems *(Green Bean Press, 1998)*
Long Live the 2 of Spades *(Green Bean Press, 2000)*
The Unclean *(Kitty Litter Press, 2002)*
Like a Fish *(Sundress Publications, 2011)*
The One Where I Ruin Your Childhood *(Sundress Publications, 2015)*
Shit House Rat *(Spartan Press, 2017)*
Gamma Rays *(CWP Press, 2018)*

Journals:

The Meadow, The Gasconade Review, Clockwise Cat, Philosophical Idiot, Joey and the Backboots, The Chiron Review, The Kentucky Review, Fried Chicken and Coffee, The Mas Tequila Review, Everyday Genius, Poetry South, The Los Angeles Review, Stirring, Juked, Full of Crow, Phoo! *(India)*, The Louisiana Review, Hobart, Drunk Monkeys, and The Rye Whiskey Review

I probably forgot a few, and I apologize.

Anthologies:

Hurricane Blues: Poems about Katrina and Rita *(Southeast Missouri State University Press, 2006)*

Daniel Crocker is a southeastern Missouri based poet and was the first winner of the Gerald Locklin Prize in poetry. He is the editor of The Cape Rock *(Southeast Missouri State University)* and the co-editor of Trailer Park Quarterly. He's also a host, with his wife Margaret Bazzell-Crocker, of the podcast, Sanesplaining. His work has appeared in The Los Angeles Review, Hobart, Big Muddy, New World Writing, Stirring, Juked, The Chiron Review, The Mas Tequila Review and over 100 others. His books include Like a Fish (full length) and The One Where I Ruin Your Childhood (e-chap with thousands of downloads), both from Sundress Publications. Green Bean Press published several of his books in the '90s and early 2000s. These include People Everyday and Other Poems, Long Live the 2 of Spades, the novel The Cornstalk Man and the short story collection Do Not Look Directly into Me. He has also published several chapbooks through various presses. His newest full-length collection of poetry, Shit House Rat, was published by Spartan Press in September of 2017.

www.ingramcontent.com/pod-product-compliance
Lightning Source LLC
Chambersburg PA
CBHW030112100526
44591CB00009B/383